More from Wei-Chuan Publishing

Cookbooks: (Bilingual: English/Chinese)

Chinese Appetizers & Garnishes
Chinese Cooking, Favorite Home Dishes
Chinese Cooking For Beginners*
Chinese Cooking Made Easy
Chinese Cuisine
Chinese Cuisine-Szechwan Style
Chinese Cuisine-Taiwanese Style
Chinese Dim Sum
Chinese One Dish Meals
Chinese Seafood*
Chinese Snacks (Revised)
Favorite Chinese Dishes
Great Garnishes
Healthful Cooking
Japanese Cuisine
Low Cholesterol Chinese Cuisine
Mexican Cooking Made Easy**
Microwave Cooking I, Chinese Style
Microwave Cooking II, Chinese Style
Noodles, Chinese Home-Cooking
Noodles, Classical Chinese Cooking
Rice, Chinese Home-Cooking
Rice, Traditional Chinese Cooking
Thai Cooking Made Easy
Vegetarian Cooking

Others:

Video-Chinese Garnishes I*
Video-Chinese Garnishes II*
Carving Tools

* English and Chinese are in separate editions

**Also available in English/Spanish

Wei-Chuan Cookbooks can be purchased in the U.S.A., Canada and twenty other countries worldwide.

Wei-Chuan Publishing
1455 Monterey Pass Road, #110, Monterey Park, California 91754, U.S.A.
Tel: (213) 261-3880 • Fax: (213) 261-3299

Cucumbers in Soy Sauce 57
Spicy Pickled Cucumbers 15
Tomato & Cucumber Salad 11

DEEP-FRYING
Deep-fried Coated Mushrooms ..56
Taro Root Cakes 55
Vegetable Cakes 54
Vegetables in Bread Crumbs 52
Vegetables in Flour Paste 53

EGGPLANT
Eggplant in Ginger Sauce 24
Stir-fried Eggplant (1) 34
Stir-fried Eggplant (2) 35

FRYING
Assorted Fried Vegetables 48
Bean Curd Skin Rolls 49

LEAFY VEGETABLES
Braised Nappa Cabbage 59
Cabbage & Tomato 40
Chinese Broccoli in Oyster Sauce .26
Chinese Leeks with Sesame Seeds .29
Gai Choy in Chicken Broth 58
Lettuce in Oyster Sauce 27
Spinach with Minced Garlic 28
Stir-fried Bok Choy 31

MUSHROOMS
Asparagus & Mushrooms 47
Baked Mushrooms with Butter 51
Chinese Pea Pods & Mushrooms ..46
Deep-fried Coated Mushrooms ..56
Lima Beans & Mushrooms 45
Mushrooms & Avocado Salad ...10
Mushrooms in Oyster Sauce 44
Mushrooms with Sesame Oil 33

OTHER VEGETABLES (BELL PEPPER, CAULIFLOWER, TURNIP, PUMPKIN, ETC.)
Bell Pepper in Black Bean Sauce .42
Cauliflower in Black Bean Sauce ..43
Chinese Turnip Salad 18
Pumpkin Cooked in Sauce 60
Stir-fried Burdock Root 39

POTATO & SWEET POTATO
Baked Sweet Potato 50
Potato Salad 13
Stir-fried Potato Shreds 38

SEAWEED
Cold Seaweed Salad 20
Stewed Seaweed 21

STIR-FRYING
Asparagus & Mushrooms 47
Bell Peppers in Black Bean Sauce 42
Braised Bamboo Shoots 37
Cabbage & Tomato 40
Cauliflower in Black Bean Sauce ..43
Chinese Pea Pods & Bean Sprouts .41
Chinese Pea Pods & Mushrooms ..46
Dry-cooked String Beans 36
Lima Beans & Mushrooms 45
Mushrooms in Oyster Sauce 44
Mushrooms with Sesame Oil 33
Stir-fried Bok Choy 31
Stir-fried Burdock Root 39
Stir-fried Eggplant (1) 34

Stir-fried Eggplant (2) 35
Stir-fried Potato Shreds 38
Stir-fried Soy Bean Sprouts 32

TARO ROOT
Taro Root Cakes 55
Taro Roots with Minced Garlic ..25

TOMATO
Cabbage & Tomato 40
Tomato & Cucumber Salad 11

Index

APPETIZERS
Bean Thread Salad 12
Chinese Turnip Salad 18
Cucumber Salad 16
Easily Pickled Vegetables 17
Mushrooms & Avocado Salad ...10
Potato Salad 13
Spicy Pickled Cucumbers 15
Tomato & Cucumber Salad 11
Vegetable Rolls 14

ASSORTED VEGETABLE
Assorted Fried Vegetables 48
Assorted Vegetables & Agar-Agar Salad 30
Bean Thread Salad 12
Easily Pickled Vegetables 17
Mushrooms & Avocado Salad ...10
Potato Salad 13
Vegetable Cakes 54
Vegetable Rolls 14
Vegetables in Bread Crumbs 52
Vegetables in Flour Paste 53

BAKING
Baked Mushrooms with Butter 51
Baked Sweet Potato 50

BAMBOO SHOOT
Braised Bamboo Shoots 37
Lima Beans & Bamboo Shoot 61

BEAN SPROUTS
Bean Curd Skin Rolls 49
Chinese Pea Pods & Bean Sprouts 41
Stir-fried Soy Bean Sprouts 32

BEANS
Boiled Soybeans in Pods 19
Chinese Pea Pods & Bean Sprouts 41
Chinese Pea Pods & Mushrooms 46
Dry-cooked String Beans 36
Lima Beans & Bamboo Shoot 61
Lima Beans & Mushrooms 45
Stewed Peanuts 22
Stewed Pinto Beans 23

BOILING
Assorted Vegetables & Agar-Agar Salad 30
Boiled Soybeans in Pods 19
Chinese Broccoli in Oyster Sauce .26
Chinese Leeks with Sesame Seeds 29
Cold Seaweed Salad 20
Eggplant in Ginger Sauce 24
Lettuce in Oyster Sauce 27
Spinach with Minced Garlic 28
Stewed Peanuts 22
Stewed Pinto Beans 23
Stewed Seaweed 21
Taro Roots with Minced Garlic ..25

COOKING IN SAUCES
Braised Nappa Cabbage 59
Cucumbers in Soy Sauce 57
Gai Choy in Chicken Broth 58
Lima Beans & Bamboo Shoot ...61
Pumpkin Cooked in Sauce 60

CUCUMBER
Cucumber Salad 16

Lima Beans & Bamboo Shoot

❶
- total of ⅔ lb. (300g): lima beans, diced bamboo shoot (or green peas, diced potato)
- ¼ c. diced ham or meat

❷
- ½ c. water
- ½ T. cooking wine
- ⅛ t. salt

❸
- 1 T. water
- 1 t. cornstarch

1. Bring ❶ and ❷ to boil. Reduce heat to medium; cover and cook for 3 minutes. Thicken with mixture ❸ and serve.

Pumpkin Cooked in Sauce

- 1 lb. (450g) pumpkin, cut in pieces
- 1 T. shredded ginger root
- ❶ 1 ¼ c. water
  1 T. ea: soy sauce, cooking wine, sugar
  ⅛ t. salt

1. Heat 1 T. oil and stir-fry ginger until fragrant. Add ❶ and pumpkin; bring to boil. Reduce heat to medium; cover and cook for 10 minutes until soft. Serve.

- Pumpkin seeds may be removed before cooking if desired.

Braised Nappa Cabbage

❶
- 1 lb. (450g) nappa cabbage
- 2 T. dried shrimp
- ½ c. dried squid
- 3 Chinese black mushrooms
- 3 slices ginger root

❷
- 1 ½ c. water
- ½ t. salt

1. Peel leaves off cabbage then cut each leaf in half. Cut dried squid in strips. Soak the mushrooms in cold water until softened then shred.

2. Heat 3 T. oil and stir-fry ❶ in the order listed until fragrant. Add nappa cabbage and stir-fry briefly. Add ❷ and bring to boil. Reduce heat to medium; cover and cook 10 minutes until cabbage is done and liquid is reduced to 1/2 c.

Gai Choy in Chicken Broth

2 lb. (900g) gai choy

2 T. shredded ginger root

❶ 1 c. chicken stock
1 T. cooking wine
¾ t. salt

❷ 2 T. water
1 ½ T. cornstarch

1. Remove stem ends then wilted leaves of gai choy; cut in pieces then rinse. Cut off leaves and retain for cooking soup, (see p.9, Figs. 36 & 37).

2. Cook remaining stems (about 1 lb., 450 g) in boiling water for 2 minutes; remove. Rinse under cold water; drain.

3. Heat 2 T. oil and stir-fry ginger root until fragrant. Add cooked stems and stir-fry briefly; add ❶ and bring to boil. Reduce heat to medium and cook 4 minutes. Thicken with mixture ❷; serve.

1 lb. (450g) cucumbers

½ T. minced garlic clove

❶
1 ½ c. water
3 T. soy sauce
1 t. sugar

Cucumbers in Soy Sauce

1. Pare cucumbers and cut into 1" (3 cm) pieces.

2. Heat 3 T. oil and stir-fry garlic until fragrant. Add cucumbers and ❶; bring to boil. Reduce heat to medium and cook 15 minutes; serve.

- Bitter gourd or winter squash may be substituted for cucumber.

⅔ lb. (300g) mushrooms

1 T. soy sauce

6 T. flour

dash of salt, pepper

oil for deep-frying

Deep-fried Coated Mushrooms

1. Remove stems from mushrooms and boil 2 minutes. Remove and mix in soy sauce; drain. Dip in flour and set aside.
2. Heat oil and deep-fry mushrooms in medium heat for 1 1/2 minutes until golden brown; remove. Sprinkle with salt, pepper as desired. Serve hot.

- Canned mushrooms may be substituted for fresh.

Taro Root Cakes

❶ total of ⅔ lb. (300g) (shredded): *taro root, onion*

❷ 1 egg
¼ t. ea: *salt, sugar*

❸ 1 T. ea: *cornstarch, flour* (or 2 T. flour)

oil for deep-frying

1. Mix ❷ well then mix in ❶ and ❸ in the order listed. Divide into 12 cakes.
2. Heat oil and deep-fry taro root cakes in medium heat for 4 minutes until crispy. Serve.

- Taro root (see p.9, Figs. 34 & 35).

Vegetable Cakes

❶ *total of ⅔ lb. (300g): onion, potato, carrot, string beans or shredded cabbage*

❷ *¼ c. water*
1 egg

½ c. flour

oil for deep-frying

1. Mix ❷ evenly then mix in ❶ and flour in the order listed. Divide into 12 cakes.
2. Heat oil and deep-fry cakes in medium heat for 4 minutes until crispy. Serve with ketchup or shaved bonito dipping sauce.

• **SHAVED BONITO DIPPING SAUCE:** Bring 3 T. cooking wine to boil; add 4 T. soy sauce, 1/2 T. sugar, and 1 c. water; bring to another boil. Add 1 c. shaved bonito; turn off heat. Let shaved bonito sink to the bottom; filter to make the sauce. When serving, add minced white radish (see p.9, Fig.33) and chopped green onion as desired for extra flavor.

Vegetables in Flour Paste

⅔ lb. (300g) of any combination of: string beans, onion, eggplant, green bell pepper, carrot, pumpkin, sweet potato, zucchini

❶
1 c. flour

½ t. baking powder

1 c. ice water

1 T. oil

oil for deep-frying

1. Cut string beans into long strips. Slice other vegetables.

2. Mix flour with baking soda well; add water and oil and mix evenly to make mixture ❶. If flour is too dry, add some water.

3. Heat oil; coat vegetables with mixture ❶ then deep-fry in medium heat for 2 minutes until golden. Serve with shaved bonito dipping sauce (see p. 54).

Vegetables in Bread Crumbs

½ onion

❶ ½ ea: green bell pepper, zucchini

¼ ea: carrot, sweet potato

❷ ¼ c. flour

1 egg, beaten

1 c. bread crumbs

oil for deep-frying

1. Cut onion into rings, secure each ring with a toothpick. Slice ❶. Coat vegetables with ❷ in the order listed. Set aside.

2. Heat oil and deep-fry vegetables in medium heat for 2 minutes until golden; serve with ketchup or other favorite dipping sauce.

Baked Mushrooms with Butter

⅔ lb. (300g) fresh mushrooms

❶ 3 T. butter
¼ t. ea: salt, pepper

1 sheet aluminum foil, 20" (50 cm) square

1. Rinse mushrooms and mix with ❶. Wrap in aluminum foil.
2. Preheat oven to 450°F (235°C); bake mushrooms for 12 minutes. Remove and serve.

Baked Sweet Potato

2 sweet potatoes (or potatoes), about 2 lb. (900g)

❶ | *6 c. water*
1 T. salt

1. Soak sweet potatoes in ❶ for 30 minutes (see p.9, Fig. 40); remove.
2. Preheat oven to 400°F (200°C) then bake sweet potatoes (do not wrap in aluminum foil) for 60 minutes until soft and chopstick can be easily poked in. Serve.

- Sweet potato tastes better if soaked before baking. If not soaked, it takes longer to bake.

Bean Curd Skin Rolls

❶ total of ½ lb. (225g): bean sprouts, shredded carrot

4 sheets of bean curd skin, 10" X 10" (24 cm X 24 cm)

❷
¼ t. salt

1 t. sesame oil

❸ 2 T. ea: cornstarch, water

2 T. soy sauce

❹ 1 t. ea: sugar, vinegar

½ t. chili oil

1. Blanch ❶ in boiling water briefly (or cook in microwave 3 minutes); remove and mix with ❷. Divide the mixture into 4 portions (filling). Mix ❸ and set aside.

2. Place a portion of filling in each bean curd skin; then fold the skin and wrap the filling to form a baton. Seal the edge of the skin with mixture ❸.

3. Heat 3 T. oil; fry bean curd rolls in low heat (to prevent burning) 1 minute until golden brown. Remove and cut in pieces; sprinkle with ❹.

Assorted Fried Vegetables

❶ *total of ⅔ lb. (300g): potato, onion, green bell pepper, eggplant*

1. Slice ❶ and set aside.
2. Heat 2 T. oil and fry potato over medium heat for 2 minutes. Add other ingredients and fry for another 2 minutes until all sides are golden brown.

- Salt and pepper may be added as desired.

Asparagus & Mushrooms

❶ total of ⅔ lb. (300g): asparagus or cucumber, red bell pepper, mushrooms, carrot

❷ 4 T. water or stock
½ T. cooking wine
¼ t. ea: salt, sugar
dash of pepper
1 t. cornstarch
½ t. sesame oil

1 Heat 1 1/2 T. oil. Add ❶ and ❷; cover and cook until steamy. Stir to mix well; serve.

- Asparagus (see p.8, Fig.26). Red bell pepper (see p.7, Figs.18-20)

Chinese Pea Pods & Mushrooms

12 Chinese black mushrooms, pre-softened in cold water

❶ 12 slices of Chinese pea pods
½ lb. (225g) mushrooms

1 T. minced garlic cloves

❷ 2 T. water or stock
¼ t. salt
dash of pepper

1. Heat 1 1/2 T. oil and stir-fry garlic until fragrant. Add mushrooms and stir-fry briefly. Add ❶ and ❷; cover and cook until steamy. Stir to mix well; serve.

Lima Beans & Mushrooms

❶ total of ⅔ lb. (300g): lima beans, mushrooms

1 T. chopped green onion

❷ 3 T. water
¼ t. salt
dash of pepper

1 Heat 2 T. oil and stir-fry green onion until fragrant. Add ❶ and ❷; cover and cook until steamy. Stir to mix well; serve.

- If using fresh lima beans, cook first then remove skin. If using frozen lima beans, soak in water then remove skin (see p.8, Fig. 25).

Mushrooms in Oyster Sauce

total of ⅔ lb. (300g): canned button mushrooms, mushrooms

1 T. chopped green onion

1 ⅓ T. oyster sauce

1 t. sesame oil

1. Heat 1 1/2 T. oil and stir-fry green onion until fragrant. Add the mushrooms; stir-fry briefly. Add oyster sauce; stir to mix well. Sprinkle with sesame oil. Serve.

Cauliflower in Black Bean Sauce

⅔ lb. (300g) cauliflower or broccoli

❶ ½ T. ea (minced): garlic clove, fermented black beans

❷
½ c. stock or water
1 T. soy sauce
⅛ t. salt
1 t. sugar, sesame oil
½ T. cornstarch

1. Remove stem then cut cauliflower in pieces (see p.7, Figs. 21-23)

2. Heat 1 1/2 T. oil and stir-fry ❶ until fragrant. Add cauliflower and mixture ❷ Cover and cook until steamy. Stir to mix well; serve.

3. Wei-Chuan's Cantonese Sauce (about 3 T.) may be substituted for the ingredients in ❷. If used, there is no need to include the ingredients ❶ in this recipe unless desired.

Bell Peppers in Black Bean Sauce

❶ *total of ⅔ lb. (300g) (cut in pieces): green, yellow, & red bell pepper, onion*

❷ *½ T. ea (minced): garlic clove, fermented black beans*

❸ 3 T. water
⅓ t. salt

1. Heat 1 1/2 T. oil and stir-fry ❷ until fragrant. Add ❶ and ❸; cover and cook until steamy. Stir to mix well; serve.

Chinese Pea Pods & Bean Sprouts

total of ⅔ lb. (300g): Chinese pea pods, bean sprouts

❶ | 3 T. water
　 | ¼ t. salt

1. Prepare and rinse Chinese pea pods (see p. 7, Fig. 24) and bean sprouts separately.
2. Heat 1 1/2 T. oil. Add pea pods and stir-fry briefly. Add bean sprouts and ❶; cover and cook until steamy. Stir to mix well; serve.

Cabbage & Tomato

❶ ⅔ lb. (300g) cabbage
½ tomato (medium size)

❷ 3 T. water
⅓ t. ea: salt, sugar

1. Cut cabbage, tomato in pieces.
2. Heat 1 1/2 T. oil; add ❶ and ❷; cover and cook until steamy. Stir to mix well; serve.

Stir-fried Burdock Root

½ lb. (225g) burdock root

❶
- 3 c. water
- 1 T. vinegar

1 T. sesame oil

3 oz. (75g) shredded beef

❷
- 2 T. ea: water, sugar
- 3 T. soy sauce

1 T. white sesame seeds, toasted

1. Use fresh, firm burdock root with moist skin. Scrape with the dull edge of a knife to pare, and wash. Cut into 1 1/2" (4 cm) sections, then shred. Soak in ❶ to prevent discoloration. Drain well before use. (Prepared, shredded burdock root may be purchased in super markets.)

2. Heat 1 T. sesame oil; add burdock root and stir-fry until dry. Remove and wipe wok dry. Heat 2 T. oil; add beef and stir-fry until color changes. Add burdock root, ❷ in the order listed and stir-fry 3 minutes until liquid evaporates. Sprinkle with toasted white sesame seeds. Serve.

- Shredded red chili may be added for people who like spicy food. This dish may also be refrigerated and served cold for a different flavor.

Stir-fried Potato Shreds

⅔ lb. (300g) potatoes

❶
- 4 T. water
- ¼ t. salt
- 1 t. minced garlic clove

1. Shred potatoes and soak in water to prevent discoloration. Drain and set aside.
2. Heat 2 T. oil. Add potatoes and ❶; cover and cook until steamy then stir-fry to mix well; serve.

Braised Bamboo Shoots

1 lb. (450g) cooked or canned bamboo shoots

6 sections green onion, 1" (3cm) long

❶
- 2 T. water
- 1 T. soy sauce
- ¼ t. salt
- 1 t. sugar

1. Cut bamboo shoots into pieces; set aside.

2. Heat 2 T. oil and fry bamboo shoots until golden brown; move aside. Add green onions and stir-fry until fragrant. Add mixture ❶ and mix in bamboo shoots; cover and cook over low heat until liquid is almost evaporated; serve.

• This dish may be served cold or hot.

Dry-cooked String Beans

⅔ lb. (300g) string beans

2 T. ground pork

❶ 1 T. ea (chopped finely): pre-softened dried shrimp, Szechuan pickled mustard greens

❷ 2 T. water
2 t. soy sauce
1 t. ea: sugar, vinegar

2 T. chopped green onions

1. Remove both ends of string beans and pull away the veins on both sides (see p.8, Fig. 31); rinse and drain.
2. Heat 4 T. oil; add string beans and fry 5 minutes until dried and wrinkled. Remove.
3. Heat 1 T. oil; stir-fry the ground pork until color changes. Add ❶ and stir-fry until fragrant. Add string beans and mixture ❷; stir to mix. Sprinkle with green onion. Serve.

Stir-fried Eggplant (2)

⅔ lb. (300g) eggplant

❶
- 1 t. minced garlic clove
- 1 t. chili or chili paste

¼ c. ground pork

❷
- 2 T. water
- ¾ T. fish sauce
- ¾ T. soy sauce
- ½ t. ea: sugar, cornstarch
- fresh basil leaves as desired

1. Cut eggplant in pieces then blanch in boiling water 1 minute; remove.
2. Heat 2 T. oil then stir-fry ❶ until fragrant. Add meat and stir-fry until color changes. Add eggplant then mixture ❷; stir to mix. Serve.

- Soy sauce may be substituted for fish sauce.

Stir-fried Eggplant (1)

⅔ lb. (300g) eggplant

❶
- ¼ c. ground pork
- 1 T. minced garlic cloves

❷
- 3 T. water
- ½ t. ea: vinegar, salt
- ½ t. ea: cornstarch, sugar
- ½ c. fresh basil leaves

oil for deep-frying

1. Cut eggplant into sections, 2 1/4" (6cm) long. Halve or quarter each section lengthwise.

2. Heat oil and deep-fry eggplant over medium heat for 2 minutes until soft. Remove eggplant and oil, leaving 1 T. oil to stir-fry ❶ briefly. Add eggplant, basil leaves, and mixture ❷. Stir to mix. Serve.

- Deep-fried eggplant is flavorful, colorful and fragrant.

Mushrooms with Sesame Oil

⅔ lb. (300g) mushrooms

10 slices ginger root

2 T. dark sesame oil

❶ ½ c. ea: water, cooking wine
⅓ t. salt

1. Rinse mushrooms; drain and set aside.
2. Heat 2 T. sesame oil then stir-fry ginger until fragrant. Add ❶ and mushrooms; cover and bring to boil. Remove and serve.

Stir-fried Soy Bean Sprouts

⅔ lb. (300g) soy bean sprouts

❶ *⅓ c. water*
1 t. cooking wine
¼ t. salt

1 Heat 2 T. oil; add soy bean sprouts and ❶. Cover and cook until steamy. Stir briefly. Reduce heat to medium; cover and cook for another 4 minutes. Serve.

- Soy bean sprouts are nutritious and delicious. May be used in soups.
- Add green onion or fresh garlic as desired for enhanced flavor.

Stir-fried Bok Choy

⅔ lb. (300g) bok choy

❶ 8 sections green onion, 1" (3cm) long
½ T. minced garlic cloves

❷ 4 T. water
¼ t. salt

1. Bok choy usually contains sand and dirt. Remove stem ends and wilted bok choy leaves; cut in pieces then rinse before use (see p.8, Figs. 28 & 29).

2. Heat 2 T. oil then stir-fry ❶ until fragrant. Add bok choy and ❷. Cover and cook until steamy. Stir briefly then cook for another minute. Serve.

- Bamboo shoots, mushrooms, and Chinese black mushrooms may be added as desired.

Assorted Vegetables & Agar-Agar Salad

❶
- ½ oz. (15g) Agar-Agar
- ⅓ lb. (150g) shredded gherkin cucumbers
- 3 oz. (75g) shredded carrots
- 3 oz. (75g) shredded ham

❷
- 1 T. ea: vinegar, sesame oil
- ½ t. salt
- 1 t. ea: sugar, minced garlic clove

1. Cut agar-agar into sections and soak in cold water 10 minutes; remove and mix with ❶ and mixture ❷. Serve.

- Agar-agar contains neither calories nor cholesterol. It is good for elderly people or people on a diet.

- Bean thread sheets may be substituted for agar-agar. Shredded chicken or pork may be used for ham. Other vegetables may also be used as desired.

Chinese Leeks with Sesame Seeds

⅔ lb. (300g) Chinese leeks*

❶ 6 c. water
1 t. salt
1 T. oil

1 T. cooked sesame seeds

dash of dried shaved bonito

❷ 1 t. ea: water, sugar
1 T. soy sauce

1. Remove wilted Chinese leek leaves then rinse.
2. Bring ❶ to boil; add leeks and cook 1 minute; remove. Rinse with cold water then squeeze out water slightly. Cut in sections and sprinkle with sesame seeds, dried shaved bonito, and ❷. Serve.

* Chinese leeks may be substituted with mushrooms, tofu, or string beans.

Spinach with Minced Garlic

⅔ lb. (300g) spinach

❶ | 6 c. water
| 1 t. salt
| 1 T. oil

❷ | 1 t. minced garlic clove
| 1 T. soy sauce

1. Remove wilted spinach leaves and cut off roots (see p.6, Fig.9); rinse with water several times before use.

2. Bring ❶ to boil; add spinach and cook 2 minutes; remove. Rinse with cold water then squeeze out water slightly. Cut in sections and serve with mixture ❷.

- If serving hot, do not rinse with cold water.

Lettuce in Oyster Sauce

⅔ lb. (300g) lettuce

❶
| 6 c. water
| 1 t. salt
| 1 T. oil

❷
| 1 T. oyster sauce or soy sauce
| 1 T. oil or sesame oil

1. Cut lettuce in half then remove the center core.
2. Bring ❶ to boil; cook lettuce 1 minute. Remove and drain. Pour ❷ over lettuce and serve.

- Other vegetables may be substituted for lettuce. If using nappa cabbage, cook for 1 1/2 minutes. If using broccoli or zucchini, cook for 2 minutes.

Chinese Broccoli in Oyster Sauce

⅔ lb. (300g) Chinese broccoli

❶ | 6 c. water
| 1 t. salt
| 1 T. oil

❷ | 1 T. oyster sauce or soy sauce
| 1 T. oil or sesame oil

1. Cut off bottom stem of broccoli. Cut broccoli into sections of desired length (see p. 7, Fig. 17).

2. Bring ❶ to boil; add Chinese broccoli and cook 2 minutes. Remove and drain. Pour ❷ over the broccoli and toss lightly before serving.

- This is a famous Cantonese dish. People favor this dish because it is delicious and easy to prepare.

Taro Roots with Minced Garlic

⅔ lb. (300g) small taro roots

❶ | 1 T. minced garlic cloves
   | 3 T. soy sauce

1. Pare the taro roots (see p.6, Figs.10 & 11). Put taro roots in water (water should cover roots); bring to boil. Reduce heat to medium; cover and cook for 25 minutes until tender (test tenderness by poking through with a chopstick). Remove and drain. Pour mixture ❶ over taro roots and serve.

Eggplant in Ginger Sauce

⅔ lb. (300g) eggplant

❶
- 2 T. soy sauce
- 1 t. sesame oil
- 2 T. minced baby ginger root

1. Pare the eggplant and cook in boiling water for about 6 minutes until tender (test tenderness by poking through with a chopstick). Tear into strips (see p.6, Figs.13 & 14). Pour on ❶ when serving. Serve hot or cold.

- If ginger is used for baby ginger root, reduce quantity because of its spiciness.

Stewed Pinto Beans

⅓ lb. (150g) dried pinto beans

❶
- 3 c. water
- 1 t. salt
- 2 T. sugar

1. Soak beans in water for 4-6 hours then drain water; or bring water to boil, turn of heat, and let soak 1 hour.

2. Bring beans and ❶ to boil. Reduce heat to low; cover and cook 1 1/2 hours to desired tenderness and liquid is almost evaporated.

- Pinto beans may be served as a breakfast, lunch dish, or snack.

Stewed Peanuts

½ lb. (225g) raw peanuts

❶
- 2 c. water
- 1 ½ T. soy sauce
- ½ t. salt
- ½ T. rock sugar or sugar
- 2 star anises

1 t. sesame oil

1. Rinse peanuts; soak in hot water for 1 hour, or bring water to boil, turn off heat, and let soak 1 hour.

2. Bring peanuts and ❶ to boil. Reduce heat to low and cook 1 hour to desired tenderness. Mix with sesame oil; serve.

Stewed Seaweed

⅔ lb. (300g) wet seaweed

❶
- 1¾ c. water
- ½ c. soy sauce
- 1½ T. cooking wine
- ⅓ t. salt
- 1 T. rock sugar or sugar
- 1 pack of spice pouch (or 1 t. Szechuan Peppercorns, ½ star anises)

1. Cut seaweed into 12″ X 2″ (30cm x 5cm) strips. Roll up each strip and secure with a toothpick (see p.6, Fig.16).

2. Bring seaweed and ❶ to boil. Reduce heat to medium and cook 15 minutes or to desired tenderness.

- The stewing sauce may be used to stew pressed bean curd or soybeans.

Cold Seaweed Salad

⅔ lb. (300g) wet seaweed shreds

❶
- 1 T. shredded ginger
- ½ T. shredded red chili
- 1 T. ea: vinegar, sesame oil
- 1 t. salt

1. Cut seaweed into strips and place in boiling water. Bring to boil then remove and drain. Place strips on a serving plate; pour ❶ over the seaweed. Toss lightly before serving. This salad may be served hot or cold.

- If dried seaweed is used, soak in cold water for 2 hours; change water constantly to remove any sliminess. Use 2 oz. dried seaweed since it expands about five times in bulk after soaking in water (see p.6, Fig.15).

Boiled Soybeans In Pods

1 lb. (450g) fresh soybeans in pods

❶ *4 c. water*
2 star anises

½ t. salt

1. Bring ❶ to boil. Add soybeans and cook 5 minutes; remove. Sprinkle with salt. Serve.

- This dish is a very delicious natural snack or appetizer.
- If frozen soybeans in pods are substituted, boil over high heat for 2 minutes and serve.

Chinese Turnip Salad

⅔ lb. (300g) Chinese turnips, peeled

❶
- 1 t. salt
- 1 T. ea: sugar, vinegar

1 t. sesame seeds

❷
- 1 T. red chili, sliced
- 1 t. ea: sesame oil, minced garlic clove

2 T. coriander

1. Pare turnips then slice; marinate in ❶ for at least 1 hour.
2. Heat 2 T. oil; stir-fry sesame seeds over low heat until fragrant. Add ❷; stir-fry briefly. Remove and mix with turnips and coriander. Serve.

Easily Pickled Vegetables

❶ *total of ⅔ lb. (300g): cabbage, white radish, carrot, gherkin cucumbers, baby ginger root*

1 T. salt

1 red chili, sliced

❷ *2 c. water*

1 t. black pepper or Szechuan peppercorns

3 cinnamon leaves (optional)

1 star anise

❸ *½ c. sugar*

½ c. vinegar

1. Tear cabbage leaves into pieces. Cut other ingredients into chunks. Marinate in salt 1 hour. Rinse briefly in cold water. Drain and set aside.

2. Boil ❷; reduce heat to low and simmer 10 minutes. Add ❸ and cook until sugar dissolves. Remove and allow to cool. Mix with ❶ and red chili; marinate for 1 day.

- This dish may be kept in refrigerator and served anytime as an appetizer.

Cucumber Salad

⅔ lb. (300g) cucumber

1 t. salt

❶
2 t. ea: vinegar, sesame oil

1 t. sugar

1 t. ea. (minced): chili, garlic clove

1. Cut off cucumber ends. Partially pare skin of cucumber. Cut in sections then pat to slightly flatten (see p.5, Figs. 4 & 6). Marinate in salt 1 hour. Drain then mix with ❶; serve.

Spicy Pickled Cucumbers

1 lb. (450g) gherkin cucumbers

1 ⅓ t. salt

1 ⅓ T. ea: sugar, vinegar

❶ total of 2 T. (shredded): ginger root, red chili

2 T. sesame oil

❷ 6 sections dried chili, ½" (1.5cm) long

1 t. Szechuan peppercorns

1 Cut off cucumber ends. Cut in sections then in strips. Remove seeds (see p. 5, Fig. 5). Marinate in salt 1 hour. Rinse cucumber with cold water; pat dry then mix with sugar and vinegar. Sprinkle with ❶.

2 Heat wok then add 2 T. sesame oil. Turn the heat to low and stir-fry ❷ until fragrant. Remove ❷ and oil. Mix with cucumber then refrigerate for 6 hours; serve.

Vegetable Rolls

3 cabbage leaves

½ lb. (225g) shredded white radish

3 oz (75g) shredded carrot

❶
1 T. ea: sugar, vinegar

1 t. sesame oil

dash of pepper

1 T. shredded baby ginger root

shredded chili as desired

1. Soften radish and carrot with 1 t. salt; marinate 20 minutes. Drain and lightly squeeze out water. Mix with ❶ and set aside.

2. Blanch cabbage in boiling water until soft. Remove and soak in cold water until cool; drain. Cut off center stems from leaves to make 6 pieces.

3. Place a portion of chili pepper, radish and carrot in each cabbage leaf, folding each end over, then rolling from the side to form a baton. Cut each roll in half (see p.5, Figs.7 & 8). Make 12 rolls.

Potato Salad

❶
- total of ⅔ lb. (300g) : green peas, diced potato & carrot
- 1 t. curry powder
- minced onion, minced coriander as desired
- 3 T. mayonnaise

1. Cook potato, carrot, and green peas. Mix with mixture ❶. Serve.

- Mushrooms and apples may be added as desired.

Bean Thread Salad

1 ¾ oz. (50g) bean threads

❶ *total of ⅓ lb. (150g): bean sprouts, shredded cucumber & carrot*

❷
½ T. soy sauce

½ T. sesame paste or peanut butter

3 T. mayonnaise

1. Mix ❷; if too thick, add some milk or vinegar.
2. Blanch bean threads in boiling water for 1 minute; remove and rinse under cold water then drain to weigh 1/3 lb. (150g). Cut bean threads into 4-inch (10cm) long sections then mix with ❶. Mix with mixture ❷ when ready to serve.

- Ham and sesame seeds may be added as desired.

Tomato & Cucumber Salad

total of 2/3 lb. (300g):
tomato, gherkin cucumbers

❶
- *1 T. vinegar or lemon juice*
- *¼ t. ea: salt, sugar*
- *dash of pepper*
- *3 T. oil*

1. Choose fresh, red, and firm tomatoes. Rinse, remove stems, then cut into pieces. Pare cucumbers then slice; briefly soak the slices in water then drain. Mix cucumbers and tomatoes with ❶ when ready to serve.

- 1/2 t. mustard, 1 t. minced onion, and 1 T. ground cucumber may be added to ❶ as desired.

Mushrooms & Avocado Salad

total of ⅔ lb. (300g): lettuce, fresh mushrooms, avocado

red & green bell peppers, shredded onion as desired

❶
- *1 T. vinegar or lemon juice*
- *¼ t. ea: salt, sugar*
- *dash of pepper*
- *3 T. oil*

1. Rinse lettuce, tear into small pieces. Slice mushrooms. Choose a ripe avocado but not too soft; remove skin and seed then cut into pieces (see p.5, Figs. 2 & 3). Mix all the vegetables with ❶. Serve.

- 1/2 T. soy sauce may be added to ❶ as desired (if so, reduce salt in ❶ slightly). Celery, coriander, minced garlic, minced ginger, etc. may also be added as desired.

33   Mashed white radish with seasoning sauce may be used as dipping sauce.

34, 35   Cut off both ends of large taro roots then remove the skins; cut in preferred shapes. They may be used to make dessert.

36, 37   Remove stem ends then wilted leaves of gai choy: cut in pieces then rinse. Cut off leaves and retain for cooking soup.

38, 39   Cut nappa cabbage in 2-inch sections then cut in pieces or shreds.

40   No need to wrap potatoes or yams in aluminum foil. Just soak in salt water before baking.

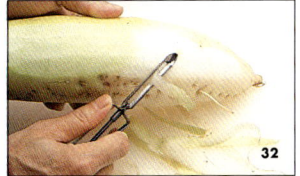

25 Skin of frozen lima beans can be easily removed without blanching. Fresh lima beans need to be blanched before their skins can be removed.

26 If the stem end of asparagus is too hard to cut, remove it.

27 Water chestnut is a frequently used ingredient in Chinese cooking. Pare off skin before use. Ready-made, canned water chestnuts are available in Chinese markets.

28, 29 Bok choy usually contains sand and dirt. Remove stem end then wilted leaves of bok choy; cut in pieces then rinse before use.

30 Dou Miao leaves are tender; may be stir-fried or cooked in soups.

31 Remove ends and veins on both sides of string beans before use.

32 Pare off skin of white radish then cut in pieces; trim into desired shape.

17	Cut Chinese broccoli into sections of desired length. Bottom stem may be used by paring off its hard skin.
18, 19, 20	Cut green or red bell peppers in half then remove seeds; cut to desired shapes. Slice one side of the piece for better presentation.
21, 22, 23	Remove stem end and leaves of cauliflower then slice or cut in pieces.
24	Remove veins from both ends of Chinese pea pods before using.

9   Spinach usually contains sand and dirt. Cut off root portion then rinse with water several times before use.

10, 11   To prepare small taro root: Cut off both ends; then pare off thick skin.

12   To prepare yellow Chinese chives and leeks: Remove withered leaves then rinse with water.

13, 14   To prepare eggplant salad: Pare off skin; cook in water until tender; tear into strips then marinate.

15, 16   Dried seaweed should be soaked in water. Change water several times during soaking until expanded to 5 times of original weight. To stew, cut soaked seaweed in wide strips; roll up the strip and secure with a toothpick then stew.

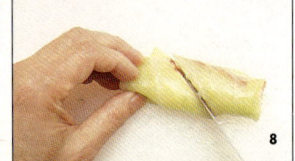

PREPARING VARIOUS VEGETABLES:

1. Mushrooms can be used in a wide variety of ways. Mushrooms which are firm and light in color should be used.

2, 3. Avocados can be pressed by fingers to determine ripeness. Cut open and remove the seed; cut into long pieces then remove skin.

4. Pare skin partially from gherkin cucumber for better presentation.

5, 6. Cut cucumber in sections then cut in strips and remove seeds; or cut cucumber in sections then pat slightly to flatten. Marinate.

7, 8. Vegetable rolls are prepared by rolling them tightly to prevent scattering when cut, (see p. 14).

Conversion Table

1 c. (1 cup) = 236 c.c.   *1 T. (1 tablespoon) = 15 c.c.*   *1 t. (1 teaspoon) = 5 c.c.*

- To prepare a meal for 2 persons, select one dish each from our Vegetable and Meat cookbooks. Complete the nutritiously balanced meal with soup or dessert.

- When stir-frying vegetables, high heat is required for satisfactory results. Therefore, do not cook too many vegetables at a time.

- Traditionally, vegetables are stir-fried in heated oil over high heat then removed immediately. Most modern kitchen stoves don't generate enough heat to cook in a traditional way, and it is hard for beginners to determine when the vegetables are done. Accordingly, stir-frying in this book is modernized by covering the vegetables in a heated, oiled pan and then cooked until steamy; stirred to mix well then removed.

- When trying a recipe for the first time, follow the instructions, timing, and quantities in the book. Recipes may be revised later according to personal preference.

Contents

Conversion Table 4

Preparing Various Vegetables 5

Appetizers 10

Boiling 19

Stir-frying 31

Frying 48

Baking 50

Deep-frying 52

Cooking in Sauces 57

Index 62

EDITOR
Huang Su-Huei
Sophia Lin

RECIPE PREPARATION
Mu-Tsun Lee
Chen Hsueh Hsia

EDITORIAL STAFF
Yen-Jen Lai
John Holt

TRANSLATOR
Wynne Chang

PHOTOGRAPHY
Aki Ohno

DESIGN
Chin Ong

ART PRODUCTION
F. Chang
Vincent Wong

PRINTING
China Color Printing Co., Inc.

WEI-CHUAN PUBLISHING
1455 Monterey Pass Rd., #110
Monterey Park, CA 91754, U.S.A.
Tel: (213)261-3880 • (213)261-3878
Fax: (213)261-3299

2nd Fl., 28 Section 4, Jen-Ai Road
Taipei, Taiwan. R.O.C.
Tel: (02)702-1148 • (02)702-1149
Fax: (02)704-2729

COPYRIGHT © 1993
By Wei-Chuan Publishing
All rights reserved.
No portion of this book may be reproduced
by any means without the permission of the
publisher.

Notice: Information contained in this book
is accurate and complete to the best of our
knowledge. All recommendations are made
with no guarantees on the part of the authors
or Wei-Chuan Publishing. The authors and
publisher disclaim all liability in connection
with the use or misuse of this information.

FIRST PRINTING, OCTOBER 1993
ISBN 0-941676-39-0

CHINESE STYLE
FAVORITE RECIPES

vegetables